ANIMALS
AT PLAY

ANIMALS
AT PLAY

Laurence Pringle

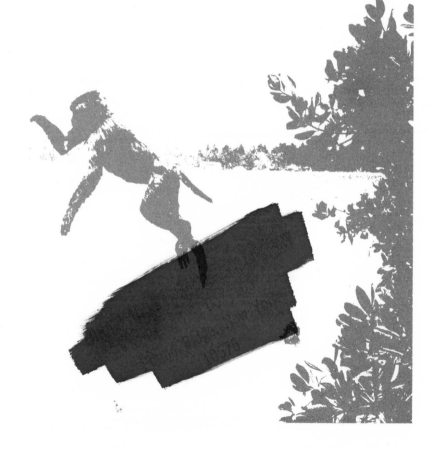

HARCOURT BRACE JOVANOVICH, PUBLISHERS

San Diego   New York   London

The quotations on pages 25, 33–34, and 52–53 are from *Animal Play Behavior* by Dr. Robert Fagen. Reprinted with permission of Oxford University Press. Copyright © 1981 by Oxford University Press, Inc.

Library of Congress Cataloging in Publication Data
Pringle, Laurence P.
   Animals at play.
   Includes index.
   Summary: An introduction to the study of the play behavior of a variety of domestic and wild animals.
   1. Play behavior in animals—Juvenile literature.
[1. Play behavior in animals. 2. Animals—Habits and behavior] I. Title.
QL763.5.P75   1985   599′.051   85-901
ISBN 0-15-203554-0

Designed by Dalia Hartman

Printed in the United States of America

First edition

A   B   C   D   E

For Jesse Erin Pringle,
a playful animal

The author wishes to thank Dr. Robert Fagen of the School of Fisheries and Science, University of Alaska, for reading the manuscript of this book and helping to improve its accuracy.

TABLE OF CONTENTS

ANIMALS AT PLAY

River otters slide down a muddy slope and splash into the water. Two ravens wheel and cavort in the sky. A kitten tussles with its mother's tail. And in a city park, one dog approaches another. It lowers its chest and head to the ground, making a bow. The second dog responds to this signal, and the dogs wrestle and chase one another until they are exhausted.

These are animals at play. Nearly all kinds of mammals and birds play when they are young, and some adults play, too. At times one species of animal will play with a different species. A fox and a deer may play chase games, or a raven may fly low over a wolf, teasing it to leap into the air.

Humans are very playful mammals, too. We play by ourselves, with other people, and with other creatures, especially our pets. We also enjoy watching other animals play. At the zoo, we look forward to the lively antics of monkeys. In fact, we have a special term for their play—monkeyshines. In our language are several other words based on animal play, including horseplay, the capers of goat kids, the gambols of lambs.

We usually recognize play when we see it, but the

A man plays with his dog in the surf. Both are very playful mammals.
Laurence Pringle

word *play* is hard to define, and scientists are somewhat puzzled by animal play behavior. Some scientists once argued that play did not merit study at all. It was, in their opinion, trivial and unimportant. Now ethologists, scientists who study animal behavior, believe that play is vital in the development of young animals.

Even though ethologists agree that animal play is important, they disagree about how it benefits animals. The study of animal play is controversial and challenging, partly because the behavior is so varied. Each kind of mammal or bird has its own way of playing. Moose play differs from parrot play. Young porcupines play in ways different from those of young vampire bats.

Nevertheless, there are some similarities in all animal play, and ways to tell play from other behavior. First, play between two animals usually begins with a signal that means "This is play." The most familiar signal is the play bow of dogs, wolves, coyotes, and other members of the canine family. A dog bows by crouching on its forelimbs, lowering its head and chest to the ground while still standing on its rear legs. Lion cubs also bow to say, "Let's play."

Play signals of other species include special tail positions and rolling on the ground. While playing, many animals also make quiet "all is well" sounds. And virtually all mammals show a relaxed, open-mouth play face whether they are playing with others or alone.

Once play begins, there are other signs that it is indeed play and is not serious. For example, fights are mock battles. The participants seldom hurt one another, as they might in a real fight. Members of the cat family usually retract their claws while playing. Young bears swat at one another but hold their paws at an angle, and their claws do not hurt their playmates. Bears, dogs, wolves, and many other mammals bite one another in play but don't use the full force of their jaws.

LEFT: A puppy play face. Virtually all mammals show a relaxed, open-mouth play face whether they are playing with others or alone.   *Marc Bekoff*

RIGHT: The play face of an adult dog.
Laurence Pringle

Playing animals restrain themselves in other ways, too. You may have seen a big dog playing with a little one. In a real fight, the big dog would win easily. In a play fight, however, the big dog does not use its full strength, so the dogs are evenly matched. Ethologists call this *self-handicapping*. They have observed this behavior in baboons, chimpanzees, and lions, among other animals. By containing its strength, a larger or older animal can lure a smaller or younger one into play. As long as the stronger one restrains its power, the match is fair and play goes on.

In a play fight, a big dog will not use its full strength against a smaller dog. *John Bishop*

Because this is play, the small dog can chase the big one. *John Bishop*

Another characteristic of play is that it seems to have no purpose other than play itself. When a kitten pounces on a piece of paper and tears it to shreds, we know that its goal is not to get food, though the skills the kitten develops may someday help it catch a mouse. The same is true of running, leaping, biting, and all the other actions of playing animals. At other times, these actions might enable an animal to catch prey or to escape an enemy. In play, these activities appear simply to provide pleasure.

Ethologists divide animal play into three categories. The first—social play—involves two or more animals in play-fighting or play-chasing. The bodies of the play-mates are often in contact. Examples of social play are young goats butting heads, elephants slapping each other with their trunks, and gorillas wrestling.

Rhesus monkeys engage in social play. Despite the expression on the face of the monkey on the left, this is a play fight, not a real one. *John Bishop*

A second category—object play—involves an individual animal playing with objects in its environment. Puppies and kittens play with all sorts of household objects, including shoes and balls of yarn. Many wild creatures play with sticks, bones, and other natural toys. Humans, however, are the only animals that actually make toys.

Object play can lead to social play. A young lion may begin to chew on an unfamiliar object which, it soon learns, is the end of its father's tail. Solo play with a stick or other object may also lead to a game of tug-of-war with a playmate.

In the third type of play—locomotor play—an individual animal performs vigorous exercise. The most common example is a leap into the air. In his book *Animal Play Behavior*, Dr. Robert Fagen of the University of Alaska at Juneau lists twenty-nine species of animals that leap vertically in play. Many of them rotate all or parts of their bodies while in the air; this is called *locomotor-rotational play*. Locomotor play also includes runs, kicks, bucks, headshakes, rolls, tumbles, bounces, spins, somersaults, jinks (quick turns), and chases of one's own tail.

LEFT: A kitten batting a telephone cord is a good example of object play. *Laurence Pringle*

RIGHT: A foal rears up, an example of locomotor play. *Robert Fagen*

Play behavior has so far been observed in 140 species of mammals and forty-five species of birds. Certain kinds of mammals and birds apparently do not play, and there is little evidence that reptiles play, although alligators and large monitor lizards have been observed manipulating objects in what may be a playful manner. One scientist claimed that she saw captive mormyrid fishes play-fighting and using objects as substitute play-mates.

Mormyrids have large brains for fish, and brain size seems to be a vital factor in the development of play behavior. The most playful species among birds and mammals have relatively large brains. Robert Fagen wrote, "Play and a highly developed cerebral cortex go together."

The possibility of play in creatures other than mammals and birds cannot be ruled out, however. It hasn't been studied much. Besides, it might be difficult for a human to even recognize play behavior in a fish or a cockroach.

There is no doubt, however, that play is an important part of the lives of most mammals and birds, and a fascinating frontier for scientists to explore.

PLAY BOWS AND OTHER CANINE SIGNALS

For as long as humans have kept dogs as pets—perhaps 14,000 years—people have had plenty of firsthand observations of animal play. Puppies spend many of their waking hours playing, and many adult dogs play, too.

The great English scientist Charles Darwin observed the play signals of his pet dog. In 1898, he described the play bow and play face of dogs. Since then other scientists have identified thirty-five different body postures, facial expressions, and gestures used in canine play. These include the *play rush,* in which an animal approaches its playmate with a bouncy gait, often moving its shoulders from side to side and using such movements as tail-wagging, head-tossing, eye-rolling, and face-pawing. Another canine play signal is two high leaps, which is called, simply enough, the *leap-leap.*

A scientist who analyzed the sounds dogs make while play-fighting and while really fighting found no differences between the growls he recorded. Body postures and facial expressions, not sounds, are the key signals that establish and maintain a play mood in dogs. Study of motion-picture films reveals slight head and eye movements that dogs direct at their playmates.

These movements suggest that dogs may have subtle play signals that are not easily detected by human observers.

The dog on the right is in the play bow position. Note also its open-mouth play face. *Marc Bekoff*

These thirty-day-old beagle puppies are already exhibiting play signals, including the play bow. *Marc Bekoff*

Besides the domestic dog, the canine family includes jackals, wolves, coyotes, dingoes, African wild dogs, and several kinds of foxes. The play of young wolves, coyotes, and beagle dogs was studied by Marc Bekoff, an ethologist at the University of Colorado at Boulder. He observed interactions between hand-raised pairs of these species when the pups were between three and seven weeks old. Bekoff found that beagle pups and wolf pups were quite playful and never fought. Their play signals were similar, although the favorite "let's play" signals of beagle pups were face-pawing and leap-leaps. Wolf pups did more head-shaking and scruff-biting as they played. Only beagle pups barked during social play; they also barked at play objects.

Coyote pups were less playful than beagles or wolves. When they were about twenty-five days old, they began the serious fights that established which animals would be dominant and which would be subordinate. This separation into leaders and followers occurs in all social mammals but begins especially early in coyotes. Among young dogs and wolves, the dominance issue is usually settled between eight and twelve weeks of age.

Once these serious fights began, there was little play between coyote pups, although they chased their own tails and indulged in other solo play. Most attempts to start play were unsuccessful, and sometimes play-fighting led to real fighting. When coyote pups did play, it was usually the result of a clear play signal given by a subordinate, a message of assurance that meant, in Marc Bekoff's words, ". . . what follows is play, and not an attempt to overthrow you."

If a coyote pup's initial play signal was rejected, it sometimes chased its own tail in an apparent effort to satisfy its need for play. When play occurred, the coyote pups wrestled, jaw-wrestled, and gave one another mock bites. Sometimes the dominant coyote of a pair would play the role of the subordinate for a while.

A wild coyote that lived on the outskirts of Lincoln, Nebraska, played with dogs. It raised its forepaw in a "let's play" signal to a golden retriever and was seen play-chasing with several different dogs. Compared with wolves and most other canines, however, coyotes are not very playful. This lack of playfulness seems to be directly related to the weak social ties that adult coyotes have with one another. They lead rather solitary lives.

In contrast, wolves are highly social mammals, usually living in groups called *packs*. The young play a

Wolves are highly social mammals. They not only play with each other, but also have been known to play with different species.   *Laurence Pringle*

great deal. Such exaggerated motions as zigzag jumps, head-tossing, and side-to-side shoulder-swaying are common play invitations. In play, wolves face-bite, scruff-bite, jaw-wrestle, ambush, and chase. They play with bones and other objects and have tug-of-wars with them. By a wild lake in British Columbia, Canada, a biologist watched five young wolves play steadily for five hours. They played with objects but mostly with one another. They chased and jaw-wrestled, and on a large stone in the water they played "king-of-the-hill" (which some people call "king-of-the-castle").

The playful wolf sometimes participates in a teasing game with ravens. In a Michigan wilderness area, biologist David Mech observed: "The birds would dive at a wolf's head or tail, and the wolf would duck and then leap at them. Sometimes the ravens chased the wolves, flying just above their heads, and once, a raven waddled to a resting wolf, pecked its tail, and jumped aside as the wolf snapped at it. When the wolf retaliated by stalking the raven, the bird allowed it within a foot before arising. Then it landed a few feet beyond the wolf and repeated the prank."

In the wild, other canines have also been observed at play with different species. In Africa, ethologists saw a family of bat-eared foxes playing a sort of chase game with a Thomson's gazelle. In Alaska, a fox seemed to be traveling with three mountain sheep rams. It jumped and bit their faces in play, and they butted the fox gently with their horns.

Marc Bekoff watched young red foxes in captivity and described three distinctive play motions: high-stepping (with the hind legs only), high-leaping (in which all four feet leave the ground), and flattening out (in which the fox lies flat on the ground and moves its head from side to side). In their overall play behavior, foxes are more like coyotes than wolves. As adults, foxes, like coyotes, do not form strong social bonds.

A high leap is a fox's invitation to play.
Marc Bekoff

The play of another wild canine, the golden jackal, was observed in Africa's Ngorongoro Crater by Baron Hugo van Lawick. He watched four pups near their den and learned to recognize individuals well enough to give them names.

Tiny head-shaking movements were the "let's play" signal of the jackal pups, and one pup was seen giving this invitation to a butterfly. In addition to romping with one another, the young jackals played with objects, tossing them and pouncing on them. Sometimes an object became a toy for all four jackal pups, as Baron van Lawick described: "One day Nugget found an ostrich feather. He sniffed it cautiously, then pounced on

13

it and began to worry it as a domestic puppy worries a slipper. When Rufus came up Nugget picked up his feather and darted away: Rufus immediately gave chase and soon their two sisters joined in as well. Round and round they raced until Rufus caught up and had a growling tug-of-war with Nugget. Suddenly Amba grabbed Nugget's tail and pulled, a favorite sport. Nugget, turning to bite at his sisters, lost the feather to Rufus. And so it went on for over an hour until only a few tattered shreds of their toy remained."

This play sounds familiar to anyone who has raised the puppies of domestic dogs. But jackals also have behavior that is unique to their kind. During play, one jackal pup would leap toward another, turn its body 180 degrees in the air, and slam its hindquarters into its playmate. These body slams are first seen in pup rough-and-tumble play. Later, as adults, jackals slam into vultures and eagles that are feeding on a dead animal, driving them away from this food source.

Baron van Lawick also saw the body slam used as a kind of greeting between two adult silverback jackals. A dominant male jackal approached another male. The high-ranking jackal quickly gave the other male two body slams and a kick, leaving the subordinate crouched in submission. Then he trotted behind a bush, only to return with a small piece of dry dung in his mouth. He set it on the ground in front of the subordinate male.

The other male made no move toward it, so the high-ranking male began to play with the dung, flinging it high in the air and trying to catch it. Hugo van Lawick wrote, "Now at last the subordinate male got up and for the next half-hour we watched as they played, chasing round and round a bush, tugging at opposite ends of twigs, jumping on to each other from a fallen tree. The offering of dung had been an invitation to play."

Like jackals and wolves, African wild dogs are highly social canines. They live in packs that roam nomadically except during the time they have pups in a den. Besides wrestling and chasing in a typical canine manner, these wild pups bite and pull the tails of their littermates and of adults. The adults tolerate this action up to a point and then will reprimand pups with quick but gentle nips on muzzles or necks. At times, though, an adult kicks backward with one leg and sends a tail-biting pup tumbling head over heels.

The amount of play among African wild dogs seems to diminish when either food or water is scarce. In times of plenty, however, entire packs play, especially after feeding and resting. Adults chase round and round, leaping over each other, sometimes turning complete somersaults in the air.

Adult African wild dogs play in a special way before a hunt. As darkness falls, the adults gather around the

African wild dogs are extremely playful, although the amount of play lessens when food or water is scarce. *SATOUR (South African Tourist Corp.)*

dominant male and excitedly lick each others' lips, wag their tails, and swirl around while making squeaking, twittering sounds. Then the wild flurry of activity ends, and the pack sets off on the hunt.

Ethologists call this behavior a *pep rally* and are curious about it. Does it help coordinate the teamwork of the pack? Does it arouse the pack members for the hunt? Is it a way for the pack leader to learn which individuals are fit and ready for hunting? Or is it a sort of physical warm-up exercise? These are some possible explanations of pep rallies, which packs of wolves often hold before hunts, too.

Wolves and African wild dogs often hold a pep rally before a hunt.
Laurence Pringle

KITTENISH

We call a playful person "kittenish," and it *is* hard to imagine anything more playful than a young cat. All cats play, not just the domestic species *Felis catus,* but also three dozen species of wild cats, ranging in size from big lions and tigers to little margays and ocelots.

Young or old, cats play by themselves, with others of their kind, with objects, and with living and dead prey. Only in the past two decades, however, have scientists studied in detail the play of domestic cats. One example is research conducted in the early 1970s by Meredith West of Cornell University's Department of Psychology.

She observed the social play of twenty-eight cats from birth up to the age of seven months. Some of these kittens were raised in a laboratory with their mothers. Meredith West also observed the behavior of fourteen kittens that lived with their mothers in her own home. She also watched, as best she could, the play of young feral cats—domestic cats gone wild.

As she watched kittens play, Meredith West faced the problem of actually identifying and describing their antics. It is easy to recognize play in a general way, but

Two Siamese kittens peer out of a bookshelf. In many ways the play of domestic cats is like that of many species of wild cats.
Laurence Pringle

what are its components? What movements, postures, and other behavior make up play? Meredith West eventually identified eight categories of motor patterns. She wrote: "The structure of social play is created through a combination of these patterns into sequences involving several patterns and involving two or more kittens."

If you have ever watched kittens play, you will probably recognize most of these postures and movements, which Meredith West called the "building blocks" of cat social play:

In the *belly-up* position, a kitten lies on its back and makes treading movements with its back legs and pawing motions with its front legs. Usually another kitten stands over it, in the *stand-up* position. It may play-bite the kitten below, or paw at it. In play two kittens frequently change roles, from stand-up to belly-up, then to stand-up again, and so on. They may also lie on their sides, pawing and treading at one another.

In the *face-off,* one kitten sitting near another hunches its body forward and looks intently toward it. The first kitten also flicks its tail back and forth and lifts a paw in the direction of the other kitten. Sometimes two kittens face-off simultaneously.

Kittens also lift both front paws off the ground and rear up into a *vertical stance,* striking out with their front paws. They make *horizontal leaps,* which begin when a kitten turns its side toward another kitten, arches its back, then leaps off the ground. This pattern is similar to the *side step,* in which a kitten arches its back, curls its tail upward, and then walks sideways toward or around another kitten.

The kitten on the right is rearing on its hind legs into the vertical stance play position. *Francesca Smith*

In its *pounce* pattern, a kitten crouches with its head low, its back legs tucked under its body and its tail straight out behind. Its tail may flick back and forth. It wriggles its hindquarters from side to side, then dashes forward. Often this leads to the eighth pattern, the *chase,* in which one kitten runs after or from another.

The findings of other scientists who have studied cat

19

play differ in some ways from the conclusions reached by Meredith West. Two British scientists, for example, divided cat play into seven categories, including play with objects, which was not listed by Meredith West because she concentrated on social play. They combined West's side step and horizontal leap into one posture, which they called *arch,* because of the prominently arched back. The action named *vertical stance* by West they called *rear; pounce* was named *stalk.*

As Meredith West watched kittens, she noticed that most play sequences began with a pounce or a side step. The pounce was the most common "let's play" signal. In the middle of a play sequence, kittens were usually in a belly-up or stand-up position. Play usually ended with a chase. Among the kittens she observed, face-offs and chases were never used to begin play.

A kitten lies in the belly-up play position beneath its mother. *Laurence Pringle*

By the fifth week, play became more complicated because three or more kittens played together. This group play was most common when kittens were about six or seven weeks old. By the time they were nine weeks old, however, nearly all play involved just two kittens again.

As the kittens grew older, their play patterns changed in other ways. At twelve weeks of age, they used fewer side steps to begin play and showed many more vertical stances than before. About the time the kittens were sixteen weeks old, they began to play less. Four-month-old cats spent more time just sitting and watching and less time with their littermates. They also did less tail-chasing and other solitary play than before. In nice weather, those kittens that were allowed outdoors spent more than four hours a day exploring and hunting.

After observing many kittens at play for two years, Meredith West concluded that the term *play-fighting* should be avoided. The term implies a great similarity between the two activities, but she found that the sequence of motor patterns is different in playing and fighting. In a real fight, cats display a defensive arched-back stance that never occurs in play. Because of this and other differences, Meredith West believes the term *play-fighting* may be misleading, particularly to those who are trying to understand why animals play.

Although kittens play less as they grow older, adult cats continue to be somewhat playful. Mothers play with their young, and adults may play during courtship. Older cats also continue to play with objects—and with prey. People often get upset when they see a cat playing

To an adult cat, a chipmunk may represent a playmate that is less threatening than another cat. *Laurence Pringle*

with a live mouse, letting it go, catching it, releasing it only to pursue it again. From a human perspective, this playing with prey looks like a bully picking on someone. People project ideas about human behavior onto the cat and say that it is being mean or cruel.

Ethologists have other ideas. Paul Leyhausen, a German authority on cat behavior, believes that some play with prey may represent a cat's caution as it tests a creature it perceives as dangerous. The cat restrains itself, approaches the prey animal hesitantly, and taps it with a paw. If the prey moves, the cat may leap back in apparent fright, especially if the prey animal is large or unfamiliar.

Leyhausen once saw an oncilla (a little spotted cat of Latin America) kill a brown rat after a hard fight. The cat then pawed, kicked, and tossed the dead rat about for a half hour. This action reminded Leyhausen of human behavior, when people celebrate wildly after successfully coming through a tense or dangerous situation. He calls this behavior *play of relief* and has observed it in several species of cat.

Behavior that Leyhausen calls *overflow play* is what seems cruel to some people, such as when a cat bats at a small animal, chases it, tosses it with its mouth, and catches it with its paws. He has observed a lynx play in this way with rabbits and chickens, a tiger with a small goat, and a lioness with young warthogs.

This sort of behavior was discussed in *Sylvie and Bruno Concluded,* written by Lewis Carroll, who was also the author of *Alice's Adventures in Wonderland.* Discussing matters with two professors, the boy Bruno claimed that a cat plays with mice to amuse them.

"But that is just what I don't know," one professor rejoined. "My belief is, it plays with them to *kill* them!"

"Oh, that's quite an *accident*!" was Bruno's reply.

There may be some truth in Bruno's statement. In the opinion of many ethologists, adult cats sometimes need to have a prey animal as a playmate. They may lack opportunities to play with others of their kind, or may be too fearful to play with the adult cats that are available.

A mouse or other prey animal is less threatening. If the mouse keeps escaping into crevices, only to be caught again, it is unwittingly being a good playmate. The cat handicaps itself; its bite is gentle because it seeks play, not food. This is not a mouse's idea of play, of course, and it usually dies because of the cat's much greater size and strength.

Compared with domestic cats, the play of other species is difficult to study, although some have been observed in the wild and in zoos. Wild species seem to play in much the same way as *Felis catus*. The stand-up and belly-up positions, for example, are key parts of play among young lynx, tigers, and European wild cats.

There are differences among cat species, however, which affect how and even where young cats play. Most kinds of cats tend to avoid water, but some do not. Tigers, fishing cats, and flatheaded cats have been seen wrestling and splashing together in water. And cheetah cubs sometimes knock one another over with a paw-slap—a movement not used by other cat species.

Adult cheetahs knock over fleeing prey with such slaps. They trip very swift prey by sticking a forepaw in front of a hind leg. They smack other prey in the side or flank with the large dewclaw of a forepaw, causing the animal to lose its balance. So it is not surprising to find young cheetahs using the paw-slap in play.

Two young cheetahs at rest with their mother. In play, cheetah cubs use paw slaps—a movement not used by other cat species— to knock one another over. As adults, they may use paw slaps to knock over fleeing prey. *SATOUR (South African Tourist Corp.)*

Margays, small spotted cats that live in Latin America, climb trees readily and hunt there, so their play also involves aerial acrobatics. At the Chicago Zoological Park (Brookfield Zoo), Robert Fagen watched two young margays at play (they were sisters, one four months old, the other eight months old). In many ways, their behavior was like that of other cats, but they also play-chased among the tree branches in their cage.

These two margays are wrestling on the ground, but the play of margays frequently takes place among the branches of trees.   *Laurence Pringle*

Robert Fagen wrote: "One margay would hang upside down 50 feet above the ground and play-bite or hit out at the other as it leapt by. These aerial leaping games evolved into elaborate exercises of margay locomotor skill. For example, the younger kitten would stand on a branch and watch as her sister prepared to leap through the air onto her. When the older kitten jumped, the younger would wait until the last possible moment to jump away, leaving her 'surprised' sister clinging precariously to the branch just vacated by the intended 'victim.'"

The play of lion cubs includes stalking, rushing, belly-up, and stand-up patterns—behavior shown by many kinds of cats—but also includes special lion characteristics. In chases, the pursuing cub swats at the legs of the second cub and tries to grasp its rump with its forepaws. Or it may put a forepaw on the other cub's shoulder and pull it down. Adult lions bring down antelope and other prey in these ways.

A young lion nuzzles an adult. The play of lion cubs includes stalking, rushing, and belly-up and stand-up patterns. *SATOUR (South African Tourist Corp.)*

The play of young cats seems to be a way to practice skills that the cat will need as an adult. Several ethologists have tried to prove or disprove this idea. One investigator found that individual domestic cats that killed the most mice when they were kittens also killed and ate the most mice as adults. In general, ethologists have found that kittens that have experience with prey grow up to be able adult predators. Given enough opportunities, however, kittens that have had no experience as predators can also become good mouse-catchers as adults.

Is the play of kittens practice for future hunts? Perhaps. But all the movements and patterns of play, in-

A lioness with cubs at Kruger National Park in South Africa. The same movements that cubs use in play may later be used to bring down prey. *SATOUR (South African Tourist Corp.)*

cluding the aerial leaps of young margays and the paw-slaps of little cheetahs, are part of adult social life, too, and may be used when two adult cats fight. It seems that the question of why cats play may not have a simple answer.

MONKEYSHINES

How do you measure fun? According to an old saying, one gauge is a barrel of monkeys. Anyone experiencing "more fun than a barrel of monkeys" is clearly having a great time. And a person doing monkey business or monkeying around is full of mischief. From these expressions in our language, it is plain to see that we consider monkeys to be symbols of carefree, lively play.

Monkeys are primates, a group of mammals that includes about 190 species of monkeys, apes, and lemurs. Humans are also primates. Although little is known about some species, it seems likely that all primates play, and the antics of several species have been closely observed in captivity and also in the wild.

From tiny tarsiers to great apes, all primates show a relaxed play face, with mouth open but teeth hidden. Judging from studies so far, the smallest primates have rather simple play behavior.

Monkeys and apes, largest of the nonhuman primates, have the most complex play behavior. Marmoset monkeys, for example, play games of hide-and-seek and peekaboo. While in view of a potential playmate, a young marmoset quickly hides, then peeks out. Or it

Marmoset monkeys, like these in the photograph, often play games of hide-and-seek.
Laurence Pringle

may dart up to another marmoset, tag it, then dash away. These play signals usually lead to chases and wrestling, in which both young and adult marmosets participate.

We usually picture monkeys playing in trees, but there are also ground-dwelling primates, and they have extraordinary play behavior. Baboons, for example, have been seen playing with several other species, including chimpanzees, vervet monkeys, bushbucks, and impalas. Baboons play-chase and also engage in rough-and-tumble wrestling, mauling, sparring, and mock-biting. Only in play do baboons give their laugh—a staccato panting noise.

The play of another ground-dwelling monkey, the patas, includes the usual bouts of wrestling but also high-speed chases over grasslands and extraordinary bounces. The usual "let's play" signal is a series of bounces made by a patas as it looks toward a potential playmate. It then runs away with the other monkey in pursuit.

During play-chases, a patas bounces in another way, hurling itself full speed against a bush or small tree. Its hands, then its feet, strike the bush, and the monkey quickly ricochets off in a new direction. A pursuing patas makes the same side-bounce. In captivity, patas bounce off the sides of their cages.

The bouncing behavior of young patas may simply look like another way to have fun. In the wild, however, adult male patas bounce up and down in the tall grass when a lion threatens the monkey troop. The bounces seem to divert the lion's attention from the rest of the monkeys. Thus the play of juveniles may become an adult lifesaving skill.

Rhesus monkeys, which are related to patas, are also ground-dwellers, although they live in the forest and do play in trees. They live in troops made up of several males and females, plus young monkeys of various ages. In captivity, some rhesus mothers have been observed playing a little game with their infants. The mother walks away, as if leaving, then stops and looks back. When the baby monkey starts to walk toward its mother, she turns her head away, seeming to ignore it. As the baby gets close, however, the mother rhesus turns to greet it.

By three months of age, a young rhesus monkey is stalking, pouncing, chasing, and wrestling with its peers. By four months, it is an extremely agile aerial acrobat. Between the ages of four and eight months, rhesus monkeys spend most of their waking hours at play.

By three months of age, a young rhesus monkey is stalking, pouncing, chasing, and, as pictured here, wrestling with its peers.   *Donald Symons*

Ethologist Donald Symons studied the play of rhesus monkeys on La Cueva, an island off southwestern Puerto Rico. He noticed that certain postures, gaits, and facial expressions preceded play and occurred only during play. The playful gaits were *gamboling,* in which a young monkey bobbed along, taking high steps, with its front and hind end alternately raised, and *staggering,* in which a monkey lurched from side to side with its head near the ground.

Their playful postures included the *head-down,* in which a monkey put its chin on the ground, left its hindquarters raised, and looked at a potential playmate. Another play posture was the *roll-onto-back.* First the monkey walked with a staggering gait, then rolled onto its back and waved its relaxed limbs in the air, often grabbing a foot with its hand.

The young rhesus monkeys also chased one another through the branches of the island's scrubby mangrove forest. One goal of their games was to cause play partners to fall. They let go and fell readily, since the ground lay only about ten feet below. Rhesus monkeys

ABOVE: A rhesus in the roll-onto-back play position   *Donald Symons*

RIGHT: Young rhesus monkeys try to make their playmates fall from the mangrove branches to the ground.   *Donald Symons*

also played a king-of-the-hill game, in which one climbed to the top of a stump and others tried to dislodge it. And the monkeys played hide-and-seek in tall grass. One monkey would run, then crouch down and freeze in that position, waiting for another to come near. Then the hiding monkey would dash away through the grass to hide again.

The water play of wild rhesus monkeys was first studied by ethologist Carol Berman on another small island near Puerto Rico. She observed a group of about eighty monkeys at a sandy ocean beach where the water was calm and less than three feet deep.

On hot, humid days, the group headed for the beach and its surrounding mangrove forest. Then the fun began as young monkeys chased, wrestled, and splashed. They swam underwater to escape a pursuing monkey or to surprise a playmate by suddenly popping to the surface. The rhesus also leaped from twenty-foot-high limbs, belly-flopping into the water.

Adult rhesus monkeys played less but did swim about. Mothers normally carry their infants against their chests, so the babies had to scramble onto their mothers' backs and ride piggyback in order to keep out of the water. With their mothers' encouragement, however, after a few weeks the young monkeys began to swim and form play groups.

Donald Symons also saw rhesus monkeys jump from mangrove branches into a pool of water. Dr. Robert Fagen recounts Symons' observations: "Frequently a

Young and old, rhesus monkeys enjoy water play. *Carol Berman*

juvenile aimed its jumps at or near another juvenile who was swimming in the water, and occasionally scored a direct hit, pushing the swimmer under the water. Sometimes both monkeys disappeared beneath the surface and reappeared in a few seconds separated by several feet."

The monkeys swam both on and beneath the surface. Symons saw juvenile monkeys jump into a pool, swim underwater for about twenty feet, then climb out on a mangrove root. The monkeys usually swam toward or away from another monkey.

In his book *Play and Aggression,* Symons writes: "When one monkey swam toward a second, sometimes one or the other ducked under the surface just before contact would have been made and swam under water. Occasionally monkey A would be seen swimming toward B; then, while still several feet from B, A would disappear under the surface and a few seconds later monkey B would suddenly disappear, suggesting that B may have been jerked under by A. Both monkeys would then reappear on the surface separated by several feet. . . . A branch at the edge of the pool sometimes became the focus for a series of displacements, as one monkey climbing toward the branch triggered a leap into the water by a second monkey on the branch, the displacer then being itself displaced by a third monkey."

Among the rhesus and some other monkey species, observers have noticed differences in the play of males and females. By six months of age, rhesus males play more actively and enthusiastically than females. The females avoid rough-and-tumble games and are chased more than they pursue.

Young rhesus monkeys hang onto branches with their feet and grapple with their hands. *John Bishop*

The same is true of the vervet monkeys of Africa. Young females play with infant monkeys and become adept at carrying and pacifying them. The young males pay little attention to the infants. They chase and wrestle. Later in their lives, the male vervet monkeys leave their families and form new social groups; the skills they develop in play may prove useful in real fights.

From his study of rhesus monkeys, Donald Symons concluded that the social play of young males is preparation for adult life. In a magazine article, he says, "Male rhesus fight each other during mating season. No wonder young males play almost three times as much as females. They're like prizefighters training for a title bout."

Some ethologists disagree. Another possible benefit of the rough-and-tumble play among rhesus males is the social bonds that form between them. In the opinion of ethologist Janet Levy and others, these bonds may be more important than actual fighting skills when the bachelor males leave their troop and set out to seek their fortune in the adult rhesus monkey world.

We know a lot about the play of rhesus monkeys, but the primates are a diverse group, and other kinds of play behavior have been observed. Lowe's guenons, which are forest-dwelling monkeys of West Africa, often play solo, carrying a rock or a branch up a tree, dropping it to the ground, then descending to repeat the process. In social play, the guenons chase and wrestle high in trees and seem to enjoy free-falling to lower branches.

Guenons also play with other species, chasing and being chased by squirrels and teasing birds called hornbills. When a flock of hornbills roosts in a big tree, juvenile guenon monkeys leap at them and shake branches, scaring them away. The monkeys wait quietly until the birds return and settle down again. Then they make another mock attack, causing the hornbills to flee once more.

Of all the nonhuman primates, apes live the longest and are the most intelligent. They are very playful. Young gibbons, orangutans, and gorillas play in complex ways, and adults take part, too. Orangutans are deliberate, slow-moving tree-dwellers. In all behavior, including play, they use the upper parts of their bodies more than their legs. Their play involves a lot of biting, grabbing, and hair-pulling. In captivity, a father orangutan was seen tickling his little daughter, and ethologists have watched captive orangutans play with chimpanzees. The chimps moved quickly and were agile climbers and jumpers, but the orangutans had greater strength. An orangutan would appear to ignore a chimpanzee's presence, then swiftly lunge, grab it, and give it playful bites. The chimpanzee couldn't escape from the orangutan's grasp.

A chimpanzee and an orangutan begin to play. The chimp jumps about quickly while the orangutan sits and grabs at its playmate. *Terry L. Maple*

Wild gorillas seldom play when they know that humans are watching. Ethologist Dian Fossey stayed near a group of silverback gorillas until they became accustomed to her presence; then she saw plenty of playful activity. Gorillas caught and dissected flies; they picked fruit and then played kicking and throwing games. One young gorilla plopped itself into the lap of a somewhat

A mother gorilla and her child sit quietly. Wild gorillas seldom play when they know that humans are watching, but ethologists have learned that gorillas are quite playful.
Laurence Pringle

older gorilla, whom Fossey called Uncle Bert. The older gorilla plucked a handful of flowers and tickled the youngster.

In her book *Gorillas in the Mist,* Dian Fossey describes what she saw when the group crossed a grassy slope dotted with trees. Uncle Bert led four other young gorillas into a square-dance type of game, using the trees as "doh-see-doh" partners. She writes:

"Loping from one tree to the next, each animal extended its arm to grab a trunk for a quick twirl before repeating the same maneuver with the next tree down the line. The gorillas, spilling down the hill, resembled so many black, furry tumbleweeds as their frolic resulted in a big pile-up of bouncing bodies and broken branches. Time and time again, Uncle Bert playfully

38

led the pack back up the slope for another go-around with the splintered tree remnants."

Unlike gorillas, chimpanzees are not shy about their play. They have been observed a great deal in the wild and in captivity, and perhaps as a result are considered the most playful of all nonhuman primates. They play tag, follow the leader, king-of-the-hill, tug-of-war, and hide-and-seek. They also laugh, wrestle and chase, tickle one another, and play games with objects. Young chimps break off leaves, branches, and fruit clusters, then wave them about, hit a partner playfully, or grapple for them. And chimpanzee mothers play peekaboo with their young and exchange tickles and nibbles with them.

In a zoo, one young chimpanzee tries to pull another from its perch. *Laurence Pringle*

Chimpanzees break off twigs and use them as tools to extract termites from their mound-homes. But only one primate shapes objects into playthings—toys—and that is the human, *Homo sapiens*. Human play, explored in the last chapter of this book, is much more varied and complex than that of chimpanzees or any other primate. There is no doubt that play is as vital to children as it is to juvenile baboons, marmosets, and other primates.

Some of the importance of play has been revealed in studies of captive rhesus monkeys. Some infants were raised without their mothers, who normally encourage their young to be more independent at about four months of age. These motherless infants clung to their fellow monkeys. Only after six months or longer did they begin to play, and their play was timid and passive.

Other young rhesus monkeys were raised by their mothers but were denied the opportunity to be with other young. When finally placed in the company of their peers, they avoided physical contact or bit the other monkeys. They were overaggressive in play and other social situations.

The most disturbed of all were young monkeys that were raised in bare wire cages and had been deprived of their mothers and playmates. They clasped their own bodies and sucked their fingers and toes. When finally allowed to meet other monkeys their age, they avoided all social contact, including play.

Although lack of play was not the sole cause of the problems of these monkeys, it was an important factor. No play makes monkeys social misfits.

BEARS AND BATS, PORCUPINES AND PARROTS

Nearly everyone has seen dogs, cats, and monkeys play, but many other warm-blooded creatures, common and uncommon, also have some sort of play behavior. Ant-eaters and armadillos, bandicoots and beavers, parrots and porcupines, wallabys and wombats all play in their own distinctive ways.

Our knowledge of the play behavior of many species is poor. It is often based on sketchy reports, not on deliberate investigations, and sometimes observers disagree. At the Chicago Zoological Park, for example, there was no doubt that Chuckles, a tame woodchuck, often played with her keepers. But observers who watched woodchuck families in laboratories and in the wild did not see a single instance of play. Woodchuck play behavior is still a puzzle.

Woodchucks are rodents. Until recently, play among rodents was considered rare, except for the play of beavers, porcupines, and a few other large species. (Beaver kits wrestle, and roll and tumble about in water; young porcupines run about, rear up, whirl in circles, wrestle, and play-bite.) Now we know that all major forms of play can be found among the rodents, which include rats, mice, voles, gerbils, squirrels, marmots, and guinea pigs.

Both rats and mice make vertical leaps, twitch their bodies vigorously, and run erratically. Young rats play intensely with one another. They charge, pounce, and wrestle; the most playful individuals seek one another out.

Ethologist Susan Wilson of the National Zoological Park in Washington, D.C., discovered something unusual in the play of another rodent, the short-tailed vole. Those voles that are born in the spring and early summer play vigorously in simple ways, nosing one another's fur, hopping about, and running in a jerky fashion. Voles born in the autumn do not play at all. The spring young, Susan Wilson discovered, secrete a scent from the back of their heads that stimulates play. When she placed some of this chemical on the fur of fall-born voles and it was smelled by other fall-born voles, they began to play. She had proved the existence of a play smell, an odor that induces play.

Play behavior has also been observed in other small mammals. They include short-tailed shrews, which turn somersaults; marsupial dasyurids, which dash about and run erratically; and such small bats as vampire bats, little brown bats, and Mexican free-tailed bats. Vampire bats are among the most agile of all bats on the ground—or ceiling—and their young play chase games and slap each other with their wings. According to one observer, free-tailed bats and other species that live in crevice hideouts "all join together for the greater part of the day or night to play and tussle, stage sham battles and pursuits, and otherwise romp in a fashion which reminds one of a litter of puppies or kittens."

In contrast to these small mammals, whales are the largest animals on earth, are long-lived social creatures, and are quite playful. However, their normal behavior in the oceans is difficult to observe and to interpret. For example, is a whale playing when it rides the bow wave of a ship?

In captivity and without training, orca whales and dolphins balance objects on their snouts or heads, dropping them only to dive and catch them again. In the wild, gray whale calves also play with balls of kelp and other objects. They cavort around their resting mothers, swimming up onto their backs and then rolling off. They frolic in bursts of air bubbles that their mothers release underwater. Up to twenty mother-calf pairs may join in play, rolling and rubbing against one another.

Some play of seals, sea lions, and walruses is also hidden from sight beneath the water surface, but these mammals do haul themselves out onto beaches, and some can be easily observed in zoos. In the Antarctic, fur seal pups were seen playing a sort of tag game with pieces of kelp seaweed. With a strip of kelp in its teeth, one pup would swim away from the others, which then pursued. When a second pup grabbed the kelp, he or she would be "it" and would be chased.

Susan Wilson watched pairs of young harbor seals in a bay. They would leap backward in a circle through the water, each seal with its nose by its partner's tail. Sometimes this paired play concluded with an entire group of harbor seals joining in a mass frolic. She reported: "This might be initiated by one seal leaping on to a rock, looking expectantly back into the water, and diving in again as soon as a companion swims beneath it. Suddenly seals all around are leaping and streaking round the rock, blowing bubbles, splashing, tossing seaweed into the air, and continually leaping out on to the rock only to tumble back into the water when another seal passes by and nudges it."

Some of these antics resemble the play of otters, which also spend much of their lives in water. Little is known about the play of sea otters, but river otters are ranked among the most playful creatures on earth. They play with objects, wrestle, and chase on land and in water, and also slide down slopes of snow or mud.

Otters are members of the diverse weasel family, which includes ferrets, mink, polecats, badgers, fishers, martens (sables), and skunks. Many are highly playful. Martens hunt in trees, and their young chase and leap

LEFT: Members of the weasel family, otters spend much of their time—including playtime—in water. *Laurence Pringle*

RIGHT: Young striped skunks hop and tumble about in play. *Laurence Pringle*

among the branches. One may ambush another, springing down from an overhead limb. In these ways the play of martens is like that of margays—two species that are not closely related but that have similar adaptations to tree-dwelling life.

In the early 1970s, two Canadian ethologists began watching the play of black bear cubs, keeping in mind that bears evolved from doglike ancestors less than twenty million years ago. They wondered whether bear and dog play are similar. J. D. Henry and S. M. Herrero observed captive bear cubs at the Calgary Zoo and wild cubs in some Canadian national parks. They concluded that although bear body structure, teeth, and eating habits have changed considerably since bears arose from canines, bear social behavior, including play, is quite similar to the social behavior of dogs and other canines.

Like dogs, bears have highly expressive ears, which

are large and mobile. A bear's ears and its facial expressions communicate information about its mood and social status. For example, ears that are flattened back against the head are a sign of aggression; crescent ears, held perpendicular to the side of the head, are a sign of submission.

During play chases between bear cubs, a fleeing cub has partially flattened ears while the chasing bear holds its ears in the crescent position. These chases usually begin when one cub walks up behind another and nips it on the flank, rump, or leg. The first bear then flees. It may also induce a chase by seizing a play object and running away with it.

Bears do not make the play bows and exaggerated approaches that are common canine play invitations. A

Drops of water fly as two polar bears rear up and swat at one another.
Laurence Pringle

bear seeking to play wears a puckered lip expression. It approaches another cub, then paws, bites, or head-butts this potential playmate, or rears up on its hind legs. Both cubs often rear up and try to knock the other off balance. They swat at one another, hitting with their footpads, not their claws. Once one cub falls, they wrestle on the ground, exchanging play bites. The cubs seize each other's muzzle, gently interlocking jaws for up to fifteen seconds at a time.

Adult bears never hold muzzles in this way, nor do they head-butt, play-nip, or claw with their hind legs. These behavioral patterns are for play only. Black bears have other movements, such as jaw-snaps and ground paw-swats, which are used in adult threat display and never during play.

Other kinds of bears have been observed playing in zoos. Polar bear mothers play with their young on land

A mother polar bear shows a play face while her cub bites her neck.
Robert Fagen

and in water, and both adults and young play with objects. Giant pandas are not true bears, but they swat and butt one another as all bears do, and also run, shake and toss their heads, and turn somersaults.

Although the play of most animals seems about the same as others of the same kind, ethologists occasionally see an individual play in a way that distinguishes it from its playmates. For example, a Czech ethologist named A. B. Bubenik watched red deer fawns running, capering, and leaping into the air. Then one fawn accidentally turned a complete somersault while butting some leafy branches. From then on, that fawn somersaulted a lot, but no other fawns learned the stunt.

Red deer are one species of playful ungulates, animals that have hoofs. Many ungulates have been tamed, so farmers and other livestock owners often see young horses, cattle, burros, sheep, goats, and pigs at play. They all run and leap, alone or with others. Piglets chase and have pushing matches; foals rear up on their hind legs and neck wrestle; calves chase, leap, kick up their heels, and butt their mothers; lambs and kids bound, buck, and run.

The play of wild ungulates is less well known. In fact, some people are surprised to learn that bulky hippopotamuses and rhinoceroses play. They do, and so do moose. Juvenile moose play-fight with bushes, with their mothers, or with other young moose. They also kick, run erratically, and splash through water.

Some of the liveliest play occurs among the group *Caprinae,* which includes sheep, chamois, mouflon, musk oxen, and mountain sheep. Many of these species live in mountainous terrain, where exceptional agility and surefootedness are needed for survival. The play of the young reflects this capability. Wild goat (ibex) kids play king-of-the-hill on rock ledges; they even leap onto and off their mothers' backs. Goat kids break into a skipping dance at the slightest stimulus, including the sight of a passing butterfly.

In the wild, several kinds of ungulates have been seen chasing birds or other creatures smaller than themselves. Zebra foals run toward birds, causing them to fly. Also, the earliest known play of all occurs among hoofed animals. Newborn calves of wildebeest and caribou can walk and run minutes after being born. They often romp around their mothers within an hour of birth. This ability raises an intriguing question: Were they also playing *before birth,* in the womb? Fetal mammals do move about vigorously in the womb; so do fetal birds inside their eggs. Whether some species play before they are born is not known.

Young zebras neck-wrestle, rear, and kick in their play fights. *SATOUR (South African Tourist Corp.)*

Although the wildebeest running in this photograph are adults, newborn wildebeest calves can also walk, run, and play soon after birth. *SATOUR (South African Tourist Corp.)*

Many mysteries remain in the study of animal play. In the definitive book on the subject, *Animal Play Behavior,* author Robert Fagen poses scores of questions. He points out numerous gaps in our understanding of mammal play and adds that we know even less about the play of birds.

Bird play has been studied very little, and some observers have had difficulty telling play from other behavior, such as courtship and bathing. Compared with mammals of similar size, birds have relatively small brains. Their brain size limits the complexity of play in many species to solo running and jumping, play with objects, and a little social play. Some young birds dart at one another and pull each other's tails.

Some large birds play more complex games. Young frigate birds, for example, snatch feathers and strands of seaweed from one another as they soar over the ocean. In captivity, juvenile barn owls run, push, and wrestle with one another and appear to reverse roles as they play. Some predatory birds play with their prey. A hawk caught a horned lark, then continued to drop and catch it again—behavior similar to the overflow play of cats.

Birds of the crow and parrot families are most playful of all. The crow family includes crows, ravens, and magpies. In Australia, ethologist Sergio Pellis studied the social play of Australian magpies. To record their movements, he used a dance notation system—the same "shorthand" used to record the movement of ballet dancers.

Mock fights were the most common kind of magpie play, with one bird trying to lightly peck another without being pecked in return. Two birds switched the roles of attacker and defender many times. Sergio Pellis also discovered that magpies have three play signals: a low, gutteral call; a bouncy walk; and an open bill, which may be similar to the open-mouth play face of dogs and other mammals.

In captivity, ravens play with objects and with each other, sometimes lying on their sides and play-fighting with their feet. Ravens pursue one another in the air, changing roles as chaser and chased. They also play with objects while flying: One bird drops an object, and a second catches it before it hits the ground. The aerial acrobatics of ravens reminded one observer of the graceful, vigorous play of river otters; he called ravens "otters of the air."

Large parrots have relatively big brains, long lives, and intricate play behavior. Macaw, kaka, African gray, blue-fronted Amazon, and kea parrots are among the species that have been studied. The play of the large

LEFT: Parrots beak-wrestle and play king-of-the-hill for the top perch.
Laurence Pringle

RIGHT: Parrots can playfully manipulate objects with their beaks and claws.
Laurence Pringle

green kea parrots of New Zealand was observed by ethologist R. Keller at the Zurich Zoo in Switzerland. Keller saw keas throw objects and catch them, and even balance objects on their feet while lying on their backs. Keas used objects to tease a partner into social play, which includes beak-wrestling, king-of-the-hill, and hide-and-seek.

Some of the intricacies of kea play as observed by Keller were described by Robert Fagen in *Animal Play Behavior:* "Young keas are true clowns. They stand on their heads and turn somersaults on branches, on the ground, and very often in deep water, where the birds may then swim around on their backs or perform pirouettes. Play also includes behaviors that exercise muscles and skills used in flight—skimming the surface of newfallen snow, or landing upside-down. The birds hang by their bills from branches, or hang upside-down, holding on with their feet. A favorite form of play makes use of a swing (a branch suspended between two parallel chains). The keas stand on the seat of the swing and set it in motion by wing flapping or by moving their center of gravity back and forth. Often, two or three birds swing together, exhibiting an astonishing degree of coordination in their joint efforts to put the swing in motion."

Although most birds may have rather simple play behavior, the antics of parrots and ravens are comparable to those of the most playful mammals, including monkeys and other primates. A barrel of parrots may be as much fun as a barrel of monkeys.

UNDERSTANDING PLAY

Miro was the only youngster in a troop of langur monkeys in India. He had no playmates. Ordinarily a troop of langurs includes several young, but all the others had died. An ethologist named Susan Blaffer Hrdy was watching the troop. She was struck by Miro's timid behavior and his dependence on his mother.

All this changed, however, whenever Miro's troop met another langur group. Miro aggressively sought playmates and wrestled with juveniles much larger than himself. He kept being trounced but came back for more. These were his only opportunities to play.

Play was obviously important to Miro, and it is vital to many other young mammals and birds. A coyote pup signals "Let's play" again and again to a potential playmate. Rejected, it chases its own tail. A cat's pent-up urge to play is released at the sight of a mouse. Two young primates compete aggressively for the chance to play with a third. And many kinds of animals handicap themselves, withholding their strength, even taking a submissive role, in order to keep playing with a smaller, weaker partner.

Animals go to great lengths to play, and they pay

In Nepal, two langur monkeys play-fight on a tree branch. *John Bishop*

dearly for it. Play is costly in terms of energy and time. When survival is at stake, play behavior is a luxury that must be restrained or given up. In the arid Southwest, burro foals usually play alone, while foals living in places that have abundant water and food can afford to spend many hours in social play.

Play can also be physically risky. Engrossed in play, young animals may not notice a predator stalking them. When young vervet monkeys play some distance from adults, they may be chased and killed by baboons. Playing animals also run the risk of injuring themselves by falling or being caught in mud or between rocks. An ethologist watching ibex kids play on rocky ledges saw several serious falls and injuries that were bad enough to cause temporary limps.

Danger of physical injury may actually inhibit play. Lambs of desert bighorn sheep normally bound and chase with great abandon. In the southern California desert, however, swift-running lambs risk bumping into spiny cholla cacti. They play less and play more cautiously than bighorn sheep lambs that live in British Columbia, Canada, where the play environment—grassy fields and sandy bowls—allows lambs to chase and cavort at full speed.

Wild lambs in the southern California desert play cautiously and reduce the risk of bumping into spiny cacti.   *Joel Berger*

Despite physical risks and loss of energy and time, many young mammals and birds play. Why? Do they play just for fun? It is impossible for humans to know what feelings another animal experiences, but birds and mammals appear to enjoy play. They seem to be experiencing pleasure.

"Just for fun," however, does not really explain the playfulness of most mammals and birds. Many kinds of animal behavior are believed to have some value in aiding the survival of a species. Play is no exception. There must be some reason—or reasons—for the antics of so many creatures.

Since ethologists have trouble agreeing on how to define the word *play*, it comes as no surprise that they disagree about *why* animals play. Some ideas have been considered and discarded. A once-popular explanation, for example, was the surplus-energy theory: Young organisms have more energy than they need for day-to-day living, so they release it through play. This is a difficult idea to prove or disprove; indeed, how do you even establish whether animals *have* excess energy?

In *Animal Play Behavior*, Robert Fagen explored several possible benefits to play. They included the theories that play is physical training that develops endurance, strength, and skills; that play helps give an animal information about itself and its environment; that play establishes or strengthens social bonds; and that play develops flexibility and inventiveness.

Testing these ideas experimentally is difficult. Most of the existing evidence is based on observations of the great diversity of animal play, including behavior described earlier in this book. Often, contrary evidence can also be found by watching different kinds of animals at play.

Play that develops or maintains endurance and physical strength seems widespread. Young animals often begin playing just after being released from confinement, as if making up for lost opportunities. They also seem to play more than usual after a period of bad weather; this is called the *raincheck effect*. Captive ibex kids do most of their running and leaping play on steep

Play can be risky—ibex kids sometimes hurt themselves, but they prefer to chase and leap about on the roughest terrain available.   *John A. Byers*

slopes, where strength and agility are needed, even though flat areas are available and could be used. They prefer the rough terrain.

These examples suggest that animal play can be a major source of physical training. However, piglets do not play in their first days of life even though their muscles are sufficiently developed for play to occur. Infant apes and humans begin to play months before they are physically mobile. And playing animals do not use certain movements and actions that they need later as adults. This evidence would seem to indicate that some benefit other than physical training must come from play.

Playing animals may develop skills needed later in life to get food, to avoid predators, and to fight. Practice makes perfect, and there is a lot of repetition in play-fighting and play-chasing. Once young animals seem to have mastered a skill, however, their play does not stop. And animals practice movements in play that are never used in their adult life. Skill practice for adult life, therefore, is not a satisfactory explanation for all play behavior.

Through play, young animals may learn about the living and nonliving things in their environment. It also gives them opportunities to compare their abilities with those of others. This kind of learning may well occur, but there is no evidence that play behavior is especially suited for such learning or that it occurs only during play. Animals cannot help learning as they play, but this is probably a side effect to play's main benefits.

A great deal of play is social, between two or more individuals. Social play requires animals to cooperate, and their cooperative skills may be used—a lot or a little—in adult life. Some ethologists say that social play exerts a force that keeps individuals and groups together.

While you would expect to find social play in wolf packs, monkey troops, and other closely allied groups made up of both adults and young, it also occurs in species that do not live in groups. Some young animals play socially but never become part of a strong cohesive group, and other kinds of animals stay together without ever playing. Among square-lipped rhinoceroses, for example, members of a social group rarely play together. Play usually occurs when members of two *different* groups meet. Play, then, is not a universal social glue, as some ethologists have claimed.

Another possible benefit of play is development of flexibility and resourcefulness. Rats raised in environments where they seldom played became narrow, impulsive, and inflexible adults. Rats raised in a varied environment where play was common became flexible and responsive to new situations. This benefit has been demonstrated in laboratories. From observations in the wild, it seems that far-ranging animals, who need to be resourceful, are usually the most playful species. These include bottle-nosed dolphins, chimpanzees, elephants, large parrots, polar and brown bears, ravens, and river otters.

Of these species, Robert Fagen wrote, "All favor a freewheeling life-style that involves frequent movement over varied terrain. Over at least part of their yearly cycle, they both cooperate and compete each day with a number of familiar individuals. Members of these species often play even as adults. Play imparts skills and flexibility required for intelligent day-to-day adjustments in the wild."

This description fits another species that has scarcely been mentioned so far, the primate *Homo sapiens*. Human play in many ways resembles that of other mammals. Children chase and wrestle, leap and tumble, and manipulate objects. A relaxed, open-mouth grin (play face) has been observed among children of many cultures around the world. And almost everyone recalls times when they practiced self-handicapping, restraining their strength or abilities in order to have a fair match with a younger brother, sister, or other playmate.

Children play peekaboo, hide-and-seek, tug-of-war, and king-of-the-hill, just as wolves, monkeys, and other

LEFT: Upon seeing her reflection in a mirror, a delighted baby responds with an open-mouth play face. *Laurence Pringle*

RIGHT: Frisbee at the beach involves object, locomotor, and social play by those most playful of all mammals, humans. *Laurence Pringle*

intelligent mammals do. But because people are by far the most intelligent beings on earth, their play is uniquely rich and complex. Humans play throughout their long life spans. They make toys, invent games, and play verbally with riddles, jokes, and other imaginative possibilities in their language.

Once language is mastered, children can agree to play at being something else: a dinosaur, a doctor, a superhero. Objects are similarly changed: A stick becomes a sword, a car becomes a spacecraft. Games with explicit rules and dramas with assigned roles can be invented, or revised, on the spot. Make-believe and fantasy play are uniquely human.

Where does human play end? Are sports and the arts, including dance, music, painting, and literature, all play? More than two thousand years ago, the Greek philosopher Plato wrote that the roots of dance lie in "the habitual tendency of every living creature to leap." Perhaps any creative act, including writing, inventing, and making a scientific discovery, represents humans at play.

Perhaps—and perhaps not. Scientists can only speculate about the possible roles of play in complex human behavior; they still face the lesser challenge of understanding the play of nonhumans. Important steps toward that goal have been made. Although different ethologists continue to advocate their favorite theories, most agree that animals probably derive several benefits from play, not just one.

The benefits of play must be great, since children and other young creatures (as well as adults of many species) devote so much time and energy to it. The term *child's play,* usually applied to a very easy task, represents a misunderstanding of how vital play is to children and other young animals.

Animal play will continue to puzzle and enchant people for many years to come, because clues to understanding human play and its importance lie in the antics of kittens, puppies, and lambs.

FURTHER READING

Barrett, P., and Bateson, P. "The Development of Play in Cats." *Behaviour,* Vol. 66, pp. 106–120 (1978).

Bekoff, Marc. "Animal Play: Problems and Perspectives." Pages 165–188 in Bateson, P. and Klopfer, P., editors, *Perspectives in Ethology.* New York: Plenum Press, 1976.

Bekoff, Marc. "Social Play Behavior." *Bioscience,* April 1984, pp. 228–233.

Berger, Joel. "Ecology, Structure, and Functions of Social Play in Bighorn Sheep." *Journal of Zoology,* Vol. 192, pp. 531–542 (1980).

Berman, Carol. "Seaside Play Is a Serious Business." *New Scientist,* March 31, 1977, pp. 761–763.

Blaffer Hrdy, Susan. *The Langurs of Abu.* Cambridge, Mass.: Harvard University Press, 1977.

Burghardt, G. and Bekoff, M., editors. *The Development of Behavior.* New York: Garland Press, 1978.

Byers, John. "Terrain Preferences in the Play of Siberian Ibex Kids." *Zeitschrift für Tierpsychologie (Journal of Comparative Ethology),* Vol. 45, pp. 199–209 (1977).

Caro, T. M. "Relations Between Kitten Behavior and Adult Predation." *Zeitschrift für Tierpsychologie (Journal of Comparative Ethology),* Vol. 51, pp. 158–168 (1979).

Darwin, Charles. *The Expressions of the Emotions in Man and Animals.* New York: Appleton, 1898.

Eaton, Randall. *The Cheetah: The Biology, Ecology, and Behavior of an Endangered Species.* New York: Van Nostrand Reinhold, 1979.

Fagen, Robert. *Animal Play Behavior.* New York: Oxford University Press, 1981.

Fagen, Robert. "Horseplay and Monkeyshines." *Science 83,* December 1983, pp. 71–76.

Ford, Barbara. "Learning to Play, Playing to Learn." *National Wildlife,* June-July 1983, pp. 13–15.

Fossey, Dian. *Gorillas in the Mist.* Boston: Houghton-Mifflin, 1983.

Fox, Michael. *Behavior of Wolves, Dogs, and Related Canids.* New York: Harper & Row, 1972.

Garvey, C. *Play.* Cambridge, Mass.: Harvard University Press, 1977.

Gianini, C. A. "Caribou and Fox." *Journal of Mammalogy,* Vol. 4, pp. 253–254 (1923).

Hall, K. R. L. "Behaviour and Ecology of the Wild Patas Monkey, *Erythrocebus patas,* in Uganda." *Journal of Zoology,* Vol. 148, pp. 15–87 (1965).

Henry, J. D., and Herrero, S. M. "Social Play in the American Black Bear." *American Zoologist,* Vol. 14, pp. 371–389 (1974).

Kleiman, D., and Collins, L. "Preliminary Observations on Scent-Marking, Social Behavior, and Play in the Juvenile Giant Panda." *American Zoologist,* Vol. 12, p. 644 (1972).

Leyhausen, Paul. *Cat Behavior.* New York: Garland Press, 1979.

McDonald, D. "Play and Exercise in the California Ground Squirrel (*Spermophilus beecheyi*)." *Animal Behavior,* Vol. 25, pp. 782–784 (1977).

Mech, L. D. *The Wolf: The Ecology and Behavior of an Endangered Species.* New York: Natural History Press, 1970.

Nash, L. T. "The Development of the Mother-Infant Relationship in Wild Baboons (*Papio anubis*)." *Animal Behavior,* Vol. 26, pp. 746–759 (1978).

Pellis, Sergio. "A Description of Social Play by the Australian Magpie *Gymnorhine tibicen* Based on Eshkol-Wachman Notation." *Bird Behaviour,* Vol. 3, pp. 61–79 (1981).

Rosenblum, L. A., and Cooper, R. W., editors. *The Squirrel Monkey.* New York: Academic Press, 1968.

Schaller, George. *The Serengeti Lion.* Chicago: University of Chicago Press, 1972.

Smith, Euclid, editor. *Social Play in Primates.* New York: Academic Press, 1978.

Suomi, S., and Harlow, H. "Monkeys at Play." *Natural History,* December 1971, pp. 72–75.

Swartz, S., and Jones, M. L. "Mothers and Calves." *Oceans,* March 1984, pp. 11–19.

Symons, Donald. *Play and Aggression: A Study of Rhesus Monkeys.* New York: Columbia University Press, 1978.

Tizard, B., and Harvey, D., editors. *Biology of Play.* Philadelphia: J. B. Lippincott Co., 1977.

van Lawick, Baron H. *Innocent Killers.* Boston: Houghton-Mifflin, 1971.

West, Meredith. "Social Play in the Domestic Cat." *American Zoologist,* Vol. 14, pp. 427–436 (1974).

Wilson, Susan. "Juvenile Play of the Common Seal *Phoca vitulina vitulina* with Comparative Notes on the Gray Seal *Halichoerus grypus.*" *Behaviour,* Vol. 48, pp. 37–60 (1974).

Wilson, S., and Kleiman, D. "Eliciting Play: A Comparative Study." *American Zoologist,* Vol. 14, pp. 341–370 (1974).

Zucker, E., and Maple, T. "Adult Male-Offspring Play Interactions With a Captive Group of Orangutans (*Pongo pygmaeus*)." *Primates,* Vol. 19, pp. 379–384 (1978).

INDEX

Page numbers in boldface refer to photographs.